BBQ
BEER
& B.S.

BBQ BEER & B.S.

FOOD TO BOWL YOU OVER

MERV HUGHES

NEW HOLLAND

Dedicated to all those people who have stepped on any sporting field at any level and given their all. Whether you win or lose doesn't matter, as long as you've given it your best shot.

That pretty much sums up my attitude to barbecuing – 'just have a go!'

Contents

INTRODUCTION

Gathering mates and family together on a weekend and firing up the barbecue in summer – is there anything better?

The simple act of cooking steaks on the barbecue gives you a good excuse to get outside, stand around, make some noise with the tongs and enjoy a couple of beers.

There is a simple, simple rule in my house when it comes to barbecue. If you don't like your meat burnt, you don't like your meat.

People can talk about rare and medium rare but, cook it! Cook it!

A lot of people might disagree with that but I like my meat cooked. Turn your burners down low and slow, slow cook it. You can just about barbecue everything…and anything.

Barbecues have come a long way since I was a boy growing up in Euroa. I really don't remember having too many steaks back then. We just used to eat sausages and rissoles – and a lot of them – at our house in Apollo Bay.

Ironically Dad didn't like to barbecue so I didn't pick up my love for barbequing from him, although he did love to cook up some rissoles. They were quick, easy and all you really needed was a loaf of fresh bread and tomato sauce. Old school all the way.

Mum's contribution was the salads. Her specialty was coleslaw but we mostly kept to the basics – lettuce and tomato. How times have changed!

Just look at the size of barbecues now. Forget the simple hot plate you used to stack with wood and light up. Now it's all about the big barbecue outdoor kitchen. Crank on the gas and away you go!

I picked up a few of my barbecue skills from my mates but most blokes like me are self-taught. It all comes down to experience. You learn from your mistakes and you watch and learn from others. All in all, as much as barbecuing has changed, some things about getting outdoors and cooking meat will never change.

You might not agree with me but blokes will always love standing around a barbecue talking crap whilst the women are inside solving the problems of the world.

Get your grill on and enjoy!
MERV

Tales from the Crease

I'll never forget the moment I learnt I would be making my international debut in 1985.

Victoria were playing India at the MCG and I had started the season well with a few wickets and at the time, the Australian side had lost a number of great players so I could see there was some opportunities there.

Back then you heard through the media first and I heard it from the assembled crowd of media as I was walking off the field. To play with Ray Bright was a dream come true.

My cricket heroes were the big three, Ian Chappell, Dennis Lillee & Rod Marsh. You can see why I was always destined to have a moustache! Growing up, these were the three guys that epitomized greatness and playing sport at the highest level. They were aggressive and didn't take a backwards step. Those three to me, and anyone around my age, were legends. You didn't know too much about cricket if they weren't your favourite players.

Allan Border gave me my nickname 'Fruit Fly'. He was king of nicknames and he gave me the name within half an hour of meeting me. He said it was a fitting name for Australia's biggest pest. I like to think it was more down to my nervous energy being around the greats.

Only a few of the guys called me Fruit Fly. After the first test match the team changed drastically so the name didn't really stick around. I've got a whole heap of nicknames. At Footscray it's Big Fella, at Victoria it was Hilly or Swerve.

You could say I was known for my physical displays of affection for my teammates. It was a conscious thing and it definitely evolved. It was something that started when I played basketball in Werribee in the late 1970's -1980's. If you got my tongue in your ear without batting me away in time then you had to shout the beers.

Out of my cricket teammates, Allan Border hated these displays of affection the most because he copped them on a regular basis but to be honest, nobody really enjoyed it much.

My Top 5 Cricket Career Memories

- My first Test match, playing for Australia against India in 1985. I took 1 for 123 and wasn't re-selected until the Ashes against England the following year (1986/1987). Although I think I remember this one for all the wrong reasons! My debut was Bob Simpson's first game as coach and Allan Border was captain. Geoff Marsh and Bruce Reid also debuted in that Test match.
- The 1989 Ashes Series in England. It was a 4-0 series win to Australia to take the Ashes. We were the underdogs. Until then, The Ashes had been held by England since 1977.
- The 1990/1991 Test Series in the West Indies. We played a 5 match Test and the West Indies won the series 2-1 with two matches drawn. The hopes were we'd take the Series for the first time since 1975-1976 but it wasn't to be. The West Indies retained the Sir Frank Worrell Trophy but we came close.
- The 1993 Ashes Series in England. Having defended The Ashes successfully at home in the 1990/1991 series, we wanted to retain them for a second consecutive series. Of the six matches schedules, Australia won 4-1 with one match drawn. I had a career-best taking 31 wickets.
- Any Test or One-Day-er played at the MCG. You can't beat it.

The Mo

More than anything, my moustache evolved through laziness. In 1985 a mate and I did a road trip around Australia. Hair cuts, razors and shaving cream were an added expense so we just let it go – for five months! When I got home there was hair everywhere. I went to the barber for a haircut and a shave and took everything off but left the moustache on. I thought I'd leave it on for awhile as a joke. Now, I'm not that superstitious but when I got back from that trip in 1985-1986, I started bowling well. I haven't been game to shave it off since. And, for the record, no...it's not insured!

AT THE BBQ

WITH

MERV HUGHES

A great Mo is the perfect barbecue accessory.

AT THE BBQ WITH MERV HUGHES

There's no such thing as an over-cooked steak.

Signature Dish

Some would say my signature dish is burnt meat. I do like my steak well done. Yeah, I get hassled for it but I don't care.

During a recent test match Heals (Ian Healy), Tubby (Mark Taylor) and Slats (Michael Slater) came to my house and I ordered in Mexican.

Sometimes you just want to sit around, have a beer and not worry about cooking. I know it's un-Australian but it's what we did!

Chef's Selection

It is an honour and a privilege to stand beside my barbecue and sample what I am cooking. I call it the chef's selection and I dedicate a portion of my cooking plate to the odd bits off the end of whatever I am cooking. You cut a little off and you offer it up to your nearest and dearest.

You've got to be invited though. If someone tries to take stuff off my barbie without permission they get whacked with the tongs.

Summer Fun

It's fair to say my barbecue gets a bit of a workout over summer. It's so easy to gather everyone and have meat and salad and sit out in the backyard and enjoy the great outdoors.

My barbecue is gas and has a bit of a story. The father of a friend of my wife Sue made it for us as a wedding gift. It's just a steel plate with burners underneath but it's great. Our barbecue was made with love.

The barbecue really is my domain. I wouldn't say I'm a whiz in the kitchen but I'll have a go. I'm not afraid to get my hands dirty. I stick to the basics like Spaghetti Bolognese and I'll do a roast every now and then.

CHAPTER ONE

CHICKEN

STICKY CHICKEN DRUMETTES

Serves 4–6

1 kg chicken drumettes
3 tablespoons soy sauce
3 tablespoons barbecue sauce
3 tablespoons honey
1 garlic clove, crushed
1 teaspoon salt
½ teaspoon pepper

Place the drumettes in a large freezer bag. Add the remaining ingredients and shake the bag to coat the drumettes. Refrigerate until needed.

Preheat the barbecue grill to medium–high heat. Cook the drumettes for 15–20 minutes, or until golden brown, crispy and completely cooked through. Keep basting the chicken with the marinade throughout the cooking process. If the drumettes begin to burn, move the wings to a cooler part of the grill or reduce the heat.

Remove from the barbecue and place on a platter to serve.

TANDOORI CHICKEN LEGS

Serves 4–6

---

250 g plain yoghurt
1 garlic clove, crushed
1 chilli, finely chopped
1½ teaspoons cumin
1 teaspoon ground coriander
1 teaspoon cinnamon
1 teaspoon paprika
1 teaspoon fresh ginger
1 tablespoon tomato paste
1 lemon, cut into wedges
10 x chicken legs
2 teaspoons garam masala
¼ bunch coriander,
roughly chopped

Place the yoghurt, garlic, chilli, cumin, ground coriander, cinnamon, paprika, fresh ginger, tomato paste and juice from half of the lemon in a large bowl and combine well.

Prepare the chicken, making two slits; one on each side of the drumsticks 1 cm deep. Place the drumsticks in a large bowl.

Add the yoghurt mixture and turn to coat well. Cover and refrigerate for at least 3 hours, overnight if possible.

Cook the drumsticks on a lightly oiled medium–high heat barbecue grill for 30–40 minutes, depending on the size of your drumsticks. Close the barbecue hood but continue to turn the drumsticks every 5 minutes. Grill the chicken until no longer pink when cut close to the bone and the juices run clear. Reduce the heat if needed to ensure the drumsticks don't overcook or burn.

Serve the drumsticks on a large platter, lightly sprinkled with garam masala and garnished with coriander and lemon wedges.

BARBECUED CHICKEN AND AVOCADO QUESADILLA

Serves 4

2 chicken breasts
1 red onion, finely sliced
1 garlic clove, finely sliced
1 avocado, cut into long,
thin slices
100 g cheddar cheese
100 g provolone cheese
8 flour tortillas
4 tablespoons barbecue rub
(see page 164)

 MERV'S TIP *These go great with hot sauce.*

Rub the chicken with combined spices until coated evenly and leave to stand for 30 minutes.

Lightly fry the onion and garlic on a oiled barbecue flatplate until golden. Remove and set aside until needed.

Add the lightly oiled chicken fillet and grill for 4–5 minutes per side (depending on thickness of the fillets), or until cooked through.

Remove the chicken from the barbecue, place on a cutting board and cut into 1 cm slices.

Place the chicken, avocado, onion, garlic and cheeses onto the flour tortillas. Cover with a tortilla.

Place on the barbecue flatplate until lightly toasted on both sides and the cheese is melted. Cut and serve warm.

CHICKEN SCHNITZEL BURGER

Makes 12

1 cup panko breadcrumbs
salt and pepper, to taste
2 eggs
500 g chicken breast fillets,
cut into pieces to fit buns
1 tablespoon olive oil
whole egg mayonnaise
2 tomatoes, sliced
1 cup baby spinach
12 slider buns of your choice

In a shallow bowl, combine the breadcrumbs, salt and pepper.

In another bowl, beat the two eggs. Dip the chicken pieces in the beaten egg, shake off excess then dip into the bread crumbs.

Prepare barbeque for direct-heat cooking. Heat until hot. Oil the grill, cook the schnitzels until golden brown for 5–6 minutes on each side.

Slice your buns in half lengthwise and toast.

To assemble your burger, spread on the mayonnaise on the bottom half of the buns, add a piece of schnitzel, a slice of tomato and the top of the bun. Hold together with cocktail stick.

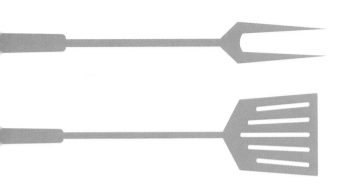

CAJUN CHICKEN ROLL WITH AVOCADO AND BACON

Makes 12

---

500 g skinless chicken thighs
1 tablespoon cumin
1 tablespoon ground coriander
1 tablespoon hot or
mild paprika
salt and pepper, to taste
2 tablespoons olive oil
6 bacon rashes
mayonnaise, to serve
2 avocadoes, sliced
1 cup arugula/rocket
12 ciabatta slider buns

Cut the chicken thighs into pieces to fit the roll. In a bowl, combine the cumin, ground coriander, paprika, salt and pepper.

In a shallow dish, layer out the chicken and drizzle with oil then sprinkle the spices over the chicken and rub in well.

Prepare barbeque for direct-heat cooking. When hot oil the grill and cook the chicken for 4–5 minutes each side until firm. While the chicken is cooking, fry the bacon on the plate of the barbeque until crispy.

Slice the buns in half lengthwise and toast them.

To assemble the rolls, dollop the bottom buns with mayonnaise, spread on some baby spinach leaves, a piece of chicken, sliced avocado and top with bacon and the bun.

CHICKEN BREAST BURGER WITH HALOUMI CHEESE

Serves 6

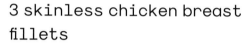

3 skinless chicken breast
fillets
2 eggplants (aubergines),
cut into 1 cm round slices
½ teaspoon salt
½ teaspoon cracked pepper
2 tablespoons barbecue rub
(see page 164)
2 tablespoons olive oil
6 haloumi slices
sweet chilli sauce, to taste
6 burger rolls of your choice
2 baby cos lettuce
3 tomatoes
1 large cucumber

Using a sharp knife, slice the chicken breast horizontally into two even pieces.

Salt each eggplant slice. Once water beads of liquid form on the surface, rinse the eggplant pieces thoroughly to remove the salt. Pat dry and spread out on a cutting board.

Combine the salt, pepper and barbecue rub.

Rub each chicken fillet with the mix and olive oil, then place on a medium–high grill. Cook for 3–5 minutes on each side, or until cooked through.

Meanwhile, place the slices of eggplant and haloumi on a medium-high oiled barbecue flatplate, turning when golden brown.

Cut the burger rolls in half and lightly toast them. Spread the base of the rolls with sweet chill sauce.

Add the chicken, eggplant and haloumi, then top with lettuce, tomato and cucumber to your liking.

CHICKEN AND VEGGIE SKEWERS

Serves 4–6

---

4 chicken breast fillets,
cut into 2 cm cubes
200 g button mushrooms
3 red onions, cut in quarters
2 yellow capsicum (peppers),
cut in to 2 cm pieces
1 x 225 g can pineapple rings,
cut into wedges
1 large lemon, cut into
thin slices

Marinade

juice and zest of 1 lemon
1 teaspoon garlic powder
1 teaspoon lemon pepper
salt and pepper, to taste
½ bunch flat-leaf parsley,
roughly chopped

Soak the skewers for 20 minutes (if using bamboo skewers).

Place ingredients onto skewers, placing the chicken, mushroom, onion, capsicum, pineapple and then fold a lemon slice and skewer. Continue until the skewer is full.

Place the skewers in a deep-sided dish or tray. Combine the marinade ingredients and coat the skewers. Leave to marinate for 5 minutes.

Cook the skewers on a medium-high barbecue grill, turning every 2–3 minutes or until cooked through.

Serve with a fresh leaf salad, if you like.

AT THE BBQ WITH MERV HUGHES

Beware of your mate that claims it's a 'chicken nugget'.

Barbecues and Backyard Cricket

In the early days, barbecues at my house weren't complete without a kick of the footy or playing backyard cricket. Nowadays kids probably play the same games on their smart phones!

Everyone has their own set of backyard cricket rules and ours were fairly standard. My Dad was a pretty handy cricketer. My brother and I used to go alright too.

We had an automatic 'wicky' (wicketkeeper). If you 'snick' the ball behind and it hit the fence, you were out.

It was six and out if you hit it over the fence.

If you hit the trees on the field – they were the fieldsmen – you were out.

Dodgy Tucker

When you're at a mate's barbecue you know the meat is going to be good. If you're with guys you don't know and the meat looks a little bit suss, you've got to careful.

A great mate of mine from school, Snapper, he's stitched just about everyone up. We went to his place for a barbecue one day and he starts handing around this plate of 'chicken nuggets'. So the boys are tucking in to these 'chicken nuggets' and there's a bit of chatter about them being a bit watery, a bit this, a bit that. We munch through a couple of plates before Snapper tells us they're not chicken nuggets but actually sweetbreads (the thymus gland [from the throat] and the pancreas gland [from the heart or stomach] from calves or lambs).

Everyone goes right off them! But I just kept on eating them.

One mate says, "You can't eat that! They taste like shit!"

I just grinned and said, "Well, I think everyone agreed they tasted alright when they were 'chicken nuggets' didn't they?"

We're always a bit wary when Snapper puts on a barbecue now. He always likes to throw in something curly for you. If he brings out a plate and you ask, 'what's this?' and he smiles...forget it!

BUTTERFLIED LEMON CHICKEN

Serves 4

1.2–1.5 kg whole chicken, cut
through the backbone
2 tablespoons worcestershire
sauce
salt
½ teaspoon cracked black pepper
1 garlic clove, crushed
juice and zest of 1 lemon
olive oil, for cooking

Put the chicken on a chopping board, breast side down, and using a pair of kitchen scissors, cut closely through each side of the backbone.

Turn the chicken breast side up and open the chicken. Place your hand on top and flatten. Rub the chicken with the worcestershire sauce, salt, pepper, garlic, lemon and olive oil.

Place the chicken on the barbecue grill, breast side down, and cook over a medium-high heat for 15–20 minutes, depending on size. Turn and cook for a further 15–20 minutes.

CHICKEN SKEWERS

Serves 4

500 g chicken breast or
thigh fillets
1 tablespoon peanut butter
2 tablespoons soy sauce
2 tablespoons lemon juice
½ teaspoon sugar
1 clove garlic, crushed
1 tablespoon sweet chilli sauce
6 spring onions
lemon and red onion slices
to garnish

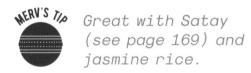 MERV'S TIP *Great with Satay (see page 169) and jasmine rice.*

Cut the chicken into 2 cm cubes. Mix the peanut butter, soy sauce, lemon juice, sugar, garlic and sweet chilli sauce to a smooth paste, adding a small amount of water if necessary to achieve a smooth consistency.

Add the chicken, mix well to cover with marinade and refrigerate for at least 30 minutes.

Meanwhile, soak 12 bamboo skewers in cold water. Peel the spring onions and cut the white section into 3 cm pieces.

Remove the chicken from the marinade and thread onto skewers, alternating chicken pieces with spring onion. Cook on the barbecue, brushing occasionally with leftover marinade, for 6–8 minutes or until chicken is cooked.

Garnish with coriander, lemon and red onions slices.

CAJUN CHICKEN AND BALSAMIC VEGETABLES

Serves 3–4

6 chicken breast fillets
4 tablespoons Cajun seasoning
2 tablespoons olive oil
balsamic vegetables
(see page 138)

Coat the chicken breast fillets with the Cajun seasoning (see page 163) and oil.

Place the chicken on a medium–high barbecue hot plate and cook for 4–5 minutes on each side, or until golden and cooked through.

Allow to rest for 5 minutes before slicing

Serve the chicken on a mound of the balsamic vegetables.

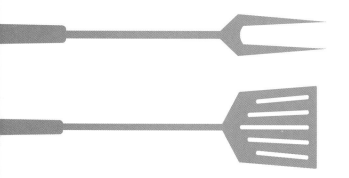

MERV'S TIP

Careful not to overcook the chicken when using the barbecue as it can get very dry.

CHICKEN WINGETTE POPS

Serves 2–4

10 chicken wingettes
(the two-bone bit, not the
little drumstick)
1 tablespoon soy sauce
½ teaspoon chilli powder
½ teaspoon cracked
black pepper
125 ml polenta
250 ml vegetable or canola oil
2 tablespoons sriracha sauce
3 tablespoons mayonnaise

MERV'S TIP *Drumettes can be used for sticky chicken drumettes recipe (see page 19). The wing tips can be kept for stock.*

Cut the wings into drumettes and the wingette pieces. For each chicken wing, push the meat down to one end and remove the thin bone. Leave the thick bone and pull the meat past the end, creating the 'lollypop'.

Combine the soy sauce, chilli and black pepper to make a marinade.

Place the chicken pops in the marinade for 30 minutes.

Dry each chicken pop on paper towel.

Place the polenta in a shallow bowl and coat each chicken pop in the polenta.

Heat the oil in a frying pan until hot (when a wooden skewer bubbles when placed in the oil). Shallow-fry the chicken pops for 3–4 minutes on each side, or until golden brown.

Combine the sriracha sauce and mayonnaise in a small serving bowl. Serve the chicken pops with the sriracha mayonnaise.

GRILLED CHICKEN WITH ORANGE

Serves 4–6

55 g butter
6 chicken joints, breasts,
thighs or Marylands (thigh
and drumsticks)
1 lemon, cut in half
salt, to taste
1 large orange, thinly sliced

Melt the butter in a small pan. Rub the chicken with half of the cut lemon, brush it liberally with melted butter and sprinkle lightly with salt.

Prepare the barbecue to medium-hot. Place the chicken, inner side up, on the grill about 10 cm above the heat.

Cook for 10–12 minutes then turn it skin side up and cook for a further 10–15 minutes, brushing with butter several times during cooking. The chicken is ready when the skin is crisp and golden and the juices run colourless when the thickest part of the flesh is pierced with a skewer.

To make the dressing, squeeze the juice from the other half of the lemon into the rest of the butter – add a little more butter if necessary. Pile the pea shoots on a platter or individual plates. Serve the chicken on top with the dressing poured over. Garnish with the orange slices.

CHAPTER TWO

SEAFOOD

FISH TACOS

Serves 6

---

1 egg
100 g plain flour
½ teaspoon salt
1 teaspoon pepper
4 fillets of any firm flesh fish
(such as snapper)
3 tablespoons olive oil
1 tablespoon butter
six 15 cm soft tacos
sweet coleslaw (see page 130)
coriander leaves, to garnish

Whisk the egg. Combine the flour, salt and pepper.

Dip the fish fillets in the egg wash, then coat the fillets in the flour mix.

Place the fish fillets on a medium–high heat barbecue flatplate with the oil and butter. Cook for 3–4 minutes on each side, or until golden brown.

Cut the fillets into long strips and place on the tacos with the sweet coleslaw. Garnish with coriander.

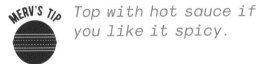 MERV'S TIP *Top with hot sauce if you like it spicy.*

BARBECUE OYSTERS WITH PARMESAN BUTTER

Serves 4–6

12 large oysters, shucked
100 g parmesan
butter (see page 175)
rock salt, to taste
lemon wedges, to serve
Tabasco sauce, to serve

Place 1 teaspoon of butter onto each oyster. Place the oysters on a hot barbecue grill and close the lid for 2–3 minutes until the butter melts. Leave to cool slightly as the shells will be hot.

Place on a serving platter scattered with rock salt to seat the oyster (so you don't lose the butter).

Serve with a few wedges of lemon and hot sauce such as Tabasco.

BARBECUED MUSSELS WITH CHILLI LIME DRESSING

Serves 4–6

about 50 fresh green-lipped mussels in the shell
fresh chives for garnish

Chilli Lime Dressing

1 clove garlic, crushed and finely chopped
¼ cup fresh lime juice
1 tablespoon Thai fish sauce
½ teaspoon prepared minced chilli
½ teaspoon brown sugar

Debeard the mussels.

Preheat the barbecue hotplate and place the muscles on top. Cook until the mussels open, covering if you have a lidded barbecue.

Discard any mussels that do not open. Break off and discard the top shell of the cooked mussels.

For the chilli lime dressing, mix the garlic, lime juice, fish sauce, chilli and brown sugar together.

Arrange the mussels on a platter and drizzle the dressing over them. Garnish with chives.

SEASONED FISH SALAD

Serves 4

¼ cup sour cream
2 teaspoons Cajun or Moroccan seasoning
4 fillets of fish
¼ cup olive oil
2 tablespoons red wine vinegar
1 tablespoon brown sugar
¼ teaspoon garlic powder
salt and pepper, to taste
1 avocado, sliced
1 red capsicum, finely sliced
½ red onion, cut into small wedges
200 g mixed lettuce
¼ cup toasted pine nuts

Combine the sour cream and seasoning and spread over the fish. Place the fish on the barbecue and grill for 5 minutes each side or until the fish is cooked through.

Whisk together the oil, vinegar, sugar, garlic powder and salt and pepper. Place the avocado, capsicum, red onion and lettuce in a bowl. Add the dressing and toss to combine. Divide the salad between serving plates, top with fish and sprinkle with pine nuts.

BACON-WRAPPED SCALLOPS WITH SPICY MAYO

Serves 4–6

12 streaky bacon strips
12 large sea scallops
½ teaspoon garlic powder
salt and pepper, to taste
lemon wedges, to serve

Spicy Mayo

60 g mayonnaise
2 tablespoons tomato sauce
1 tablespoon hot sauce
2 lemons (juice of half a lemon
for the sauce and half
to squeeze on before cooking)

Cook the bacon on a barbecue flatplate so it is about half cooked through, then leave to cool.

Wrap each scallop with a slice of bacon and secure it with a toothpick or short skewer. Squeeze over the lemon and garlic powder, then season with salt and pepper.

Cook the bacon on a hot barbecue grill until it is sizzling and the scallops are opaque.

Meanwhile, make the spicy mayo. Mix together the mayonnaise, tomato sauce, hot sauce and lemon juice in a bowl. Refrigerate until needed.

Serve the scallops while still warm with lemon wedges and spicy mayo.

PRAWN AND CHORIZO SKEWERS

Serves 6

———

1 kg green prawns, peeled,
tails on
3 chorizo sausages, cut into 1
cm pieces
coriander, to garnish
1 lemon, to serve

Prawn Marinade

1 red chilli, finely sliced
1 garlic clove
3 tablespoons olive oil
juice of 1 lemon
¼ teaspoon salt
½ tablespoon pepper

To make the prawn marinade, combine all of the ingredients.

Marinate the prawns for 5 minutes.

Soak skewers for 20 minutes, if you're using bamboo skewers, before threading the prawns and chorizo alternately on the skewers.

Cook the skewers on a medium–high grill for 2–3 minutes on each side.

Squeeze the lemon on the skewers then garnish with coriander and serve warm.

ANGELS ON HORSEBACK

Serves 4–6

---

12 large oysters, freshly
shucked or from a bottle
6 streaky bacon strips
lemon wedges, to serve

Cut each slice of bacon in half and wrap the oysters in bacon. Overlap the ends, securing with a toothpick or short skewer.

On hot grill, cook until the bacon is crisp (depending on the thickness of your bacon). Serve while warm with a wedge of lemon.

MERV'S TIP

Soak the toothpicks or skewers in water for 20–30 minutes.

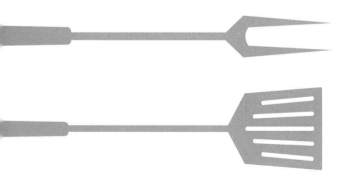

DEVILS ON HORSEBACK STUFFED WITH BLUE CHEESE

Serves 4–6

12 large dates, deseeded
100 g blue cheese, crumbed
10 streaky bacon strips

Using a knife, cut a lengthwise slit into each date to open and remove the seed (if you don't have deseeded dates).

Fill each date with blue cheese. Cut each slice of bacon in half and wrap the dates in the bacon. Overlap the ends and secure with a toothpick or short skewer.

Cook the bacon on a hot barbecue grill until crisp (depending on the thickness of your bacon). Serve warm.

AT THE
BBQ
WITH
MERV HUGHES

Keep it simple with seafood.

Something Fishy

I'm a pretty keen fisherman but not too many of my fishing conquests end up on my grill. But if I'm lucky and I get out there and get a few – whether it be snapper or flathead – I like to cook them on the barbecue – quite simply.

I reckon a lot of people spoil the fish by putting too many herbs, garlic, chilli, sauces, marinades or whatever on there. But you don't need to. You don't taste the fish.

So it's quite easy, if I have a snapper and it's on the barbecue, I wrap it in aluminium foil and cook it whole. You just clean it up and gut it. There's no need to scale it, just throw it in the aluminium foil, cook it whole, open it up when it's cooked, peel the skin back and get into the meat!

Gone Fishing

A lot of cricketers do enjoy fishing. It's well documented. Mates like Roy (Andrew Symonds), Haydos (Matthew Hayden) enjoy their fishing. And there's Andy Bichel, Michael Kasprowicz, Matthew Wade, Cameron White and Darren Pattinson – they're mad keen fishos.

Now I played probably six or seven years with Tubby (Mark Taylor) and we never spoke about fishing. And when we finished playing we both found out we had a love of fishing. So when we meet up now, we don't talk about the cricket, we don't really talk about anything but fishing!

Tubby has been on some great fishing trips. He goes up to Channel Point in the Northern Territory. I'm looking for the invitation but you know, it hasn't come my way yet.

I have a mate called Squizzy up in Darwin. He had a shack down on Bynoe Harbour. I usually go up there and chase some, Mullaway and Mangrove Jacks or whatever comes up.

I love doing the Barra Classic down on the Daly river to try to catch some Barramundi there. Uh, the elusive Barramundi, I will say, it's a lot of fun. There's a lot of hard work but when you get a good fish it's well worth the effort.

BARBECUE TUNA SKEWERS

Serves 4–6

---

4 tuna steaks, cut into 3 cm cubes
sweet coleslaw, to serve (optional, see page 130)

Marinade

4 tablespoons olive oil
1 teaspoon chilli flakes
1 teaspoon brown sugar
1 lime or lemon juice and zest (whichever you prefer)
¼ teaspoon black pepper

To make the marinade, combine all of the ingredients.

Marinate the tuna in the marinade for 10 minutes. Place the tuna on short skewers (soak the skewers for 20 minutes if using bamboo).

Preheat the barbecue grill to a medium–high heat. Place the skewers on the grill and baste with the leftover marinade to keep moist. Turn every 3–5 minutes. Cook until done to your liking.

Serve with sweet coleslaw or red Asian slaw and grilled asparagus.

SPICY BARBECUED BABY OCTOPUS

Serves 4–6

---

1 kg baby octopus
400 ml red wine
100 ml balsamic vinegar
1 garlic clove, crushed
50 ml soy sauce
50 ml hot sauce
50 ml barbecue sauce
50 ml tomato sauce
salt and pepper, to taste
20 g chopped fresh coriander,
to garnish
1 lemon, cut into wedges

Place the octopus, red wine and balsamic vinegar in a saucepan and bring to the boil over medium heat. Reduce to a simmer for 15 minutes.

Drain the octopus, then place in a large bowl. Combine the garlic, soy sauce, hot sauce, tomato sauce and barbecue sauce. Add to the octopus and mix to ensure the octopus is well coated.

Cook the octopus on a hot barbecue grill side, while basting with the sauce, for about 5 minutes or until charred. Do not over cook or they will be chewy.

When cooked, place on a serving plate with lemon and garnish with coriander.

SALMON FILLET WITH ASIAN DRESSING

Serves 4

---

4 salmon fillets
2 carrots, cut into matchsticks
2 sticks of celery, cut into matchsticks
100 g bean sprouts
2–3 spring onions, thinly sliced
coriander, roughly chopped, to garnish

Dressing

1 garlic clove, crushed
1 tablespoon soy sauce
125 ml rice vinegar
3 tablespoons caster sugar
125 ml olive oil
½ teaspoon toasted sesame oil
½ teaspoon salt
1 teaspoon freshly ground pepper

Combine all of the dressing ingredients and place in saucepan over medium heat. Stir until the caster sugar has dissolved and the mixture has thickened slightly. Allow to cool for 15 minutes.

Place the salmon fillets, skin side down, on a medium–high flatplate and cook for 3–4 minutes or until the skin is crispy. Turn the fillets over and cook until the salmon is cooked to your liking (about 2–3 minutes depending on the thickness of the fillets).

Combine the dressing and carrots, celery, beansprouts and spring onions.

Mound the vegetables and place a salmon fillet on top. Garnish with coriander.

STUFFED SQUID TUBES, PRAWNS AND COUSCOUS

Serves 4

olive oil

1 onion, finely diced

½ red capsicum (pepper), diced

2 garlic clove, crushed

2 red chillies, deseeded and finely sliced

100 g pine nuts, toasted

1 teaspoon mixed herbs

500 g cooked small prawns

4 large squid tubes (cleaned)

juice of 1 lemon

2 tablespoons chopped flat-leaf parsley

370 g cooked couscous

salt and cracked pepper, to season

Heat the olive oil in a frying pan over medium heat. Gently fry the onion, capsicum, garlic and chillies until soft and lightly coloured.

Add the pine nuts, mixed herbs and prawns and cook for 2–3 minutes.

Remove from the heat and stir in the lemon juice, parsley and couscous to form a thick, coarse mixture.

Fill each squid tube approximately three-quarters full of mixture and secure the ends with a toothpick.

Brush with olive oil and cook on a barbecue grill for 3–5 minutes on each of the four sides, depending on size of tubes.

Serve with a leafy salad.

OYSTERS IN WHITE WINE

Serves 4–6

---

48 freshly shucked small
Pacific oysters, in the shell
1 cup white wine
2 tablespoons chives, chopped
1 teaspoon pink peppercorns,
rinsed and roughly crushed
250 g salted butter, in 2 cm
cubes

Check the oysters are grit free – but try not to rinse under running water as you will lose that saltwater flavour of freshly shucked oysters.

Boil the wine and simmer for 2 minutes; add the chives and peppercorns and simmer for a further minute. Remove from the heat and swirl in the butter to melt and combine well.

Put the oysters, onto the open barbecue grill. Spoon over some of the sauce. When the liquid is bubbling, the oysters are ready to serve.

Lift the oysters from the barbecue and place them onto heaped rock salt on a platter to keep the oysters upright, or on finely shredded outer lettuce leaves for the same purpose. Leave to cool so they can be picked up and easily slipped out of the shell.

WHOLE SNAPPER IN FOIL

Serves 2

———

1 medium snapper per two people
(allow approximately 250–300 g
of fish per person)

½ teaspoon black cracked pepper

½ tablespoon fish sauce

1 tablespoon soy sauce

1 lime, sliced, plus extra
to serve

1 lemongrass stem, cut in half

2–3 spring onions, finely
chopped

1 small chilli, finely sliced

¼ bunch basil leaves, roughly
chopped (reserve some for
garnish)

¼ bunch coriander, roughly
chopped (reserve some for
garnish)

2–3 tablespoons olive oil

2 carrot, cut into matchsticks

1 celery stalk, cut into
matchsticks

2 spring onions, finely chopped

125 ml sesame oil

1 lime

Rinse the fish inside and out under running water. Pat dry with paper towel. Make three cuts 2½ cm apart, roughly 1 cm deep in thickest part of fish on each side.

Rub the pepper, fish sauce and soy sauce into both sides of the skin of the fish and place the lime slices, lemongrass stalk, spring onions, chilli, basil and coriander inside the cavity of the fish. Drizzle both sides of the fish with olive oil.

Place a sheet of foil with a piece of baking paper roughly the size the fish in the middle (this will stop the skin sticking to the foil). Place the fish on the paper and foil. Cover the fish with another sheet of baking paper and foil then fold in the sides to enclose, ensuring the fish is well sealed.

Place the fish on the barbecue grill (medium heat) and close the lid for 10–15 minutes. Turn and cook for a further 10 minutes on the other side, depending on the size of your fish (may need longer if you barbecue doesn't have a lid).

Remove from the barbecue and carefully unwrap only the top layer. Test the fish is cooked using a fork, seeing if it flakes apart easily.

Place on a serving platter. Sprinkle the carrot, celery and spring onions over the fish. Heat the sesame oil until just smoking, then carefully pour the oil over the fish. Serve with the reserved coriander, basil and the lime slices.

GRILLED FLATHEAD

Serves 4

---

4 flathead (500–600 g each)
2 tablespoons sumac spice
4 tablespoons olive oil
bunch of fresh dill
2 lemons
8–12 wooden skewers, soaked
for 30 minutes

Ask the fish monger to clean and gut the fish and remove the head. Cut off the fins and trim the tail with a pair of kitchen scissors. In a small bowl mix together the olive oil and the sumac. Slice the lemons. Wash the dill and trim off the stalks.

Place the fish on their backs on a chopping board. Into each fish cavity place a good handful of dill and 2–3 slices of lemon, then pour on some of the oil and sumac mix. With 2–3 small wooden skewers, fasten together the fish so dill and lemon do not fall out during cooking.

Turn the fish over and rub the oil and sumac mix well into the fish.

Prepare the barbeque for direct-heat cooking. Oil the grill bars well. Cook the fish on each side for 8–10 minutes. Serve with mixed salad.

BARBECUED FISH BURGER

Serves 4

---

4 fillets of firm white fish
(approximately 125 g each)
4 tablespoons Thai-style
seafood seasoning
4 round Turkish pide
90 g butter, softened
200 g green salad mix or
shredded lettuce
4 tablespoons sweet
chilli sauce
2 large tomatoes, sliced
225 g traditional tartare sauce
2 tablespoons finely chopped
spring onions
dill sprigs, to garnish

Place the fish fillets on a plate. Sprinkle both sides with seasoning. Cut the pide bread in half. Spread lightly with the butter. Prepare the filling ingredients. Take all to the barbeque area.

Prepare the barbeque for direct-heat cooking. Heat to medium-high heat. Grease the grill bars well. Brush the fish with oil, place on the grill bars and cook for 3 minutes each side or until cooked through.

Place the pide on the barbeque, crust side down, to heat a little, turn butter side down to lightly toast.

To assemble, place the lettuce on the base of each portion of pide bread, drizzle very lightly with the chilli sauce if desired. Top with 3 tomato slices. Place on the grilled fish, top with tartare sauce and sprinkle with chopped spring onion and a sprig of dill. Place on the top piece of pide.

CHAPTER THREE

BEEF

BARBECUE MEATBALL SKEWERS

Serve 4–6

oil, for cooking
1 onion, finely diced
500 g beef mince
1 egg
2 bacon rashers, finely diced
1 tablespoons barbecue sauce
1 tablespoons Worcestershire sauce
1 garlic clove, crushed
50 g (1¾ oz) panko breadcrumbs
salt and black pepper, to season

If using bamboo skewers, soak in water for 20 minutes.

Heat some oil in a frying pan over medium heat. Add the bacon and the onion then cook until the onion is soft and golden.

Combine the remaining ingredients, ensuring that it is well combined, then roll into golf size balls.

Place four balls on each skewer. Place the skewers on a medium–high barbecue flatplate and cook for 8–12 minutes or until golden brown, turning every few minutes to brown all sides.

Serve with salad and coleslaw or place the meatballs on a long bread roll with some caramelised onion relish (see page 178).

FLANK STEAK TACOS

Serves 4–6

1 kg flank steak
3 tablespoons barbecue rub
(see page 164)
2 tablespoons olive oil
1 tablespoon apple cider
vinegar
6 x 15 cm soft tacos
coriander, to garnish
1 lime, cut into wedges,
to serve
1 jalapeño, finely sliced
(optional)

Salsa

1 red onion, diced
2 tomatoes, diced
¼ bunch coriander, roughly
chopped
juice of 1 lime
salt, to season

Rub the flank steaks with the barbecue rub and place in a bowl or plastic bag with the olive oil and vinegar allow to marinate for at least 30 minutes at room temperature (overnight in the fridge will give better results).

To make the salsa, combine the onion, tomatoes, coriander, lime juice and salt, to taste, in a bowl. Refrigerate until needed.

Cook the steaks on a medium–high barbecue grill for 3–4 minutes on each side for medium rare–medium, or to your liking.

Rest for 4 minutes, then slice into strips against the grain.

While the steak is resting, warm the soft taco on the grill (on low or turned off, depending on the heat of your grill).

Serve the tacos with the flank steak and salsa and some lime wedges on the side. Garnish with coriander. Add extra jalapeños if you are game.

BLUE CHEESE STUFFED HAMBURGER

Serves 5

1 tablespoon butter
1 brown onion, finely diced
1 garlic clove, crushed
1 kg beef mince
½ teaspoon salt
½ teaspoon cracked pepper
1 teaspoon worcestershire
sauce
1 tablespoon barbecue sauce
30 g panko breadcrumbs
1 egg
100 g blue cheese
(cut into five 20 g slices)
5 soft burger bun of your
choice, halved
1 baby cos lettuce
2–3 tomatoes, sliced
aïoli or caramelised onions,
to serve

Melt the butter in a frying pan over medium heat. Add the onion and garlic and sweat until golden. Allow to cool.

Combined the mince, onion and garlic, salt, pepper, worcestershire sauce, barbecue sauce, panko breadcrumbs and egg in a bowl. Mix by hand until well mixed. Separate the mix into five equal balls.

Separate each ball again into two equal balls and place a piece of blue cheese into the centre and mould into a patty. Flatten and ensure each patty is well sealed around the edges.

Place the patties on a medium–high barbecue flatplate and cook the patties for 3–4 minutes on each side or done to your liking.

Spread the top half of the burger bun with aïoli or caramelised onion. Add the patty, then the lettuce leaves and tomato.

Serve hot (but make sure you warn everyone about the hot cheese filling).

DELUXE HAMBURGERS

Serves 10

Burger Patties

1 kg ground beef

1 large onion, grated or processed

½ cup dried breadcrumbs

½ teaspoon salt

¼ teaspoon pepper

3 tablespoons tomato ketchup

2 tablespoons water

Buns and Suggested Fillings

10 hamburger buns

softened butter for spreading

1 lettuce, separated into leaves, washed and drained

1 bunch rocket, washed and drained

2 large onions, thinly sliced and cooked on the hotplate

sandwich cheese slices

1 cup tomato ketchup

Combine all the ingredients for the burger patties. Knead by hand to distribute evenly and make the texture finer.

Rest for 20 minutes in the refrigerator. With wet hands, shape into 10 flat patties about 8 cm in diameter.

Prepare barbeque for direct-heat cooking. Heat until hot. Oil the grill bars, place on the patties and cook for 5–6 minutes on each side. Brush with a little oil as they cook.

Split the buns and lightly spread with softened butter. Place buttered side down on hotplate and toast to golden colour.

To assemble, place a lettuce leaf on bottom half of bun, top with cooked patty, tomato ketchup, onions, cheese slice, rocket leaf and your choice of pickle or relish. Top with remaining bun.

BEEF SLIDERS WITH CHEESE

Makes 12

---

1 tablespoon butter
1 small onion, finely diced
1 clove garlic, minced
500 g best-quality ground/
minced beef you can afford
1 egg
1 teaspoon Dijon mustard
1 teaspoon Worcestershire
sauce
salt and pepper
1 tablespoon olive oil
iceberg lettuce, sliced
3—4 slices cheese (Swiss or
Tasty)
2 tomatoes, sliced
pickles
whole egg mayonnaise
12 slider buns of your choice

Prepare barbecue for direct-heat cooking. Heat until hot. Melt the butter on the barbeque plate, cook the onion and garlic until golden then allow to cool.

Place meat in a large bowl and mix in the cooked onion, garlic, egg, Worcestershire sauce and season with salt and pepper. Roll into small balls and flatten the patties to fit your buns.

Prepare barbecue for direct-heat cooking. Heat until hot. Oil the grill bars, place on the patties and cook for 5–6 minutes on each side. Brush with a little oil as they cook.

Slice the buns in half lengthways.

Spread the bottom halves of the buns with mayonnaise, add some lettuce, a cooked patty, a slice of cheese, tomato and cucumber and the top of the bun. Hold the buns together with cocktail sticks and serve while hot.

Winning The Ashes 1989

One of the best days of my life was when we won The Ashes in '89 and we had a big, big celebration after the last test match. It was a 4-0 series win for Australia. We had gone into the series as complete underdogs. England had held the Ashes since the 1977 Ashes series. Our victory marked the beginning of Australia retaining the Ashes for 16 years until the Poms eventually won them back in the 2005 Ashes series.

Our sponsors (XXXX) organised a venue for a rooftop barbecue. We all jumped on a bus and we were taken to a building that looked like Gotham City. It was dark, it was dingy and most of us were just sitting there on the bus, looking at each other thinking 'This is going to be a short day! This joint looks like hell!'

We got up to the top floor and stepped out onto the roof and we couldn't believe it! This place was just like paradise. There were big palm trees, ferns and plants everywhere – you would never have imagined it from looking at the front of that building. We had a big, big barbecue that day! There were steaks, chicken, lamb, pork – basically whatever you wanted. It was great. As you know, the summer days are long in England. So we were still celebrating at 10.30pm and then some. It was still daylight so it was easy to lose track of time a bit!

The Diet

You might find it hard to believe – I know I do – but I've had a bit of a weight issue all my life. Throughout my career, former Australian cricketer and coach, Bobby Simpson (Simmo) was on my back about my weight.

At one of Swampy's (Geoff Marsh) barbecues, Simmo was just sitting there at the dinner table, watching everything I was putting into my mouth. The next morning at training he came up to me and said, "I watched you last night. You sat down and had a rissole, a piece of steak and lots of salad. That was great. As you know, we've been putting a little bit of pressure on you and your weight." Swampy was standing there next to me as Simmo was singing my praises about my food choices and the lack of quantity of food – in his eyes. Simmo walked away and Swampy looked at me and laughed, "Are you going to tell him or not?"

"Probably not..." I replied. As Swampy was cooking the barbie, I was standing next to him and I reckon I would have had 15 sausages and a few chicken wings before sitting down to eat my steak and rissole. I was just pulling them off the barbecue and Simmo had no idea. And he was praising me for that! I almost felt guilty.

AT THE
BBQ
WITH

MERV HUGHES

No celebration is complete without a sausage on the grill.

BACON-WRAPPED MEATLOAF BURGER

Serves 6–8

---

1 tablespoon butter
1 brown onion, finely diced
1 garlic clove, crushed
500 g beef mince
250 g pork mince
1 egg
30 g panko breadcrumbs
2 tablespoons barbecue sauce
1 teaspoon worcestershire sauce
1 teaspoon cumin
1 teaspoon chilli powder
¼ tablespoon salt
½ tablespoon cracked black pepper
12 streaky bacon slices

Melt the butter in a non-stick frying pan over medium heat. Add the onion and garlic and cook until soft and golden.

Place the beef and pork mince in a large bowl along with the onion and garlic, egg, breadcrumbs, barbecue sauce, worcestershire sauce, cumin, chilli powder, salt and pepper. Mix until all combined.

Shape the mixture into a loaf and wrap with the bacon slices including the ends. Place on a medium high barbecue hot plate with the ends of the bacon slices down and cook for 5–10 minutes, turning until it is brown on all sides. Baste with barbecue sauce every 5 minutes for a further 30–35 minutes.

Serve with leafy green salad or cut the loaf into slices and make burgers.

FLANKEN CUT SHORT BARBECUE RIBS

Serves 4–6

1½ kg flanken cut short ribs
½ cup barbecue rub (see page 164)
1 tablespoon olive oil
½ cup barbecue sauce
(see page 172)

Rub the ribs, ensuring they are well coated with the dry mixture. Place the ribs in a single layer on a tray. Cover and refrigerate for at least 2 hours (overnight is better).

Place the ribs on a oiled hot to medium barbecue grill. Cook for 6 minutes on each side, then reduce the heat to low. Brush with the barbecue sauce on each side until sticky and well coated with the sauce.

Rest for a few minutes before serving.
Serve with sweet potato wedges and a salad.

STEAK AND BLUE CHEESE ON TURKISH BREAD

Serves 4

---

500 g flank steak
salt and freshly ground pepper,
to taste
4 Turkish buns
200 g blue cheese, crumbed
4 tablespoons mayonnaise
2 cups coleslaw (see page 130)

Preheat the barbecue grill plate to high heat. Season the steak with salt and pepper on both sides.

Place the steak on the grill and cook to your liking. Remove the steak from the grill and rest it while toasting the ciabatta on the grill.

Slice the steak across the grain. Butter one side of the toasted ciabatta with mayonnaise. Top with coleslaw, then the sliced steak and some crumbed blue cheese. Top with the other slice of ciabatta. Serve immediately.

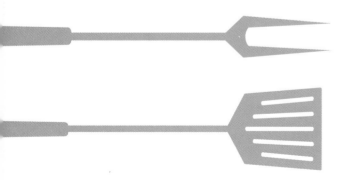

RIB EYE WITH CHIMICHURRI

Serves 4

---

4 rib eye fillets, on the bone
salt and black pepper,
to season
1 small red chilli, finely
sliced, to garnish

Chimichurri

½ bunch coriander, leaves
finely chopped
½ bunch flat-leaf parsley,
finely chopped
2 garlic cloves, crushed
1 green chilli, finely diced
juice and zest of 1 lemon
3 tablespoons olive oil

Preheat the barbecue grill plate to high heat. Season the steaks with salt and pepper on both sides.

Place the steaks on the grill and cook to your liking.

To make the chimichurri, combine the coriander, parsley, garlic, green chili, lemon juice and zest and oil in a bowl.

Serve the steaks with the chimchurri and a sprinkle of red chilli.

MERV'S TIP

A hint for the uneducated and inexperienced, if you want a good steak, you only turn your meat once. A lot of people turn it two or three times — forget it! Just turn it once.

T-BONE AND HERB BUTTER

Serves 4

—

4 large T-bone steaks
olive oil, for cooking
salt and pepper, to season
parmesan, garlic and parsley
butter (see page 175)

Remove the steaks from the fridge and leave for 20 minutes to come to room temperature.

Brush the steaks with olive oil and season with salt and pepper. Cook on a medium-high barbecue for 3–4 minutes on each side for a rare to medium steak, or until cooked to your liking.

Serve the steaks with a slice of the parmesan, garlic and parsley butter.

 MERV'S TIP *Sweet potato wedges and sweet coleslaw as sides would go well with these steaks.*

BEEF SATAYS

Serves 4

---

1 skirt steak, about 700 g
2 tablespoons vegetable oil
1 tablespoon lime or lemon
juice
salt and pepper, to taste
½ cup of satay sauce
(see page 169)
juice of ½ lemon
1 tablespoon peanut oil
20 long satay sticks, soaked
for 1 hour in cold water

Place the skirt steak on a chopping board. Remove any membrane. With a large knife lightly score the surface in a diagonal criss-cross pattern on both sides. This has a tenderising effect as it cuts through the meat fibres; it also speeds up absorption of the marinade.

Mix the oil, lime juice, salt and pepper together. Place the steak in a flat, non-metallic dish. Pour in the oil mixture, turn the meat to coat both sides. Marinate for 2 hours, turning once. Remove from the marinade, pat dry and place on a cutting board. Slice the steak across the grain, with knife held at a 45-degree angle to the meat. Strips should be about 12 cm long, 2 cm wide and 3 mm thick.

Weave the strips onto the soaked satay sticks. Arrange the skewers in a non-metallic at dish, a lasagna dish for example. Combine the lemon juice, satay sauce and peanut oil to form a marinade. Pour over the skewers. Marinate for 30 minutes.

Prepare the barbecue for direct-heat cooking, high heat. Oil the grill bars well. Slip a double foil band under the exposed part of the skewers to protect them from burning. Arrange the satays and cook for 1–2 minutes per side.
Serve immediately.

CHAPTER FOUR

PORK & LAMB

BEER-MARINATED LAMB RACK

Serves 4–6

1–3 racks (allow 3 –4 chops per person)
200 ml pale ale, or your beer of choice
1 tablespoon brown sugar
1 rosemary sprig
salt, to season
1 tablespoon cracked black pepper

MERV'S TIP *This recipe goes well with leafy or Greek salad.*

Combine the ale, sugar, rosemary and salt and pepper and mix until the sugar is dissolved.

Place lamb in the marinade for at least 30 minutes at room temperature (1–2 hours would be better with the meat at room temperature for the last 30 minutes).

Remove the racks from the marinade and pat dry with paper towel.

Grill the lamb rack, fat side down, for approximately 5 minutes on a medium–high temperature with the lid open.

Turn the lamb rack over and cook for an additional 5 minutes for medium–rare with the lid down. Cook for longer if you like your lamb cooked more, or the racks you have are bigger.

Remove from the grill and rest for 5 minutes, then cut into individual chops. Serve immediately.

BARBECUE FLATTENED LAMB LEG AND SMASHED POTATOES

Serves 6

1.5 kg lamb leg
2 garlic cloves, crushed
1 rosemary sprig, roughly chopped
2 tablespoons roughly chopped thyme leaves
3 tablespoons olive oil
½ tablespoon paprika
salt and black pepper, to season
3 lemons (1 to juice and 2 cut in half to garnish)
smashed potato recipe (see page 146), to serve

Cut the lamb from the bone and cut to spread out flat (ask your butcher to do this to save time).

Combine the lamb and all of the ingredients except the lemon halves in a large zip-lock bag. Leave to marinate for at least 4 hours (overnight is better).

Remove the lamb from the bag and using skewers, flatten out the lamb for cooking.

Place the lamb on a medium barbecue grill, turning every 5 minutes, and cook for approximately 25–30 minutes for medium-rare or until cooked to your liking.

Remove and cover with foil. Allow to the lamb to rest for 10 minutes before slicing.

Slice the lamb and place on a serving dish with the potatoes and grilled lemon halves. Squeeze the lemon onto the lamb at the table just before serving.

LAMB BACKSTRAP WITH SWEET POTATO CHOPPED SALAD

Serves 4–6

3 lamb backstraps
400 g rocket leaves and mixed leaves
2 sweet potatoes, cut into 1 cm cubes (to be roasted)
2–3 small beetroot, cooked and cubed
1 small red onion, finely sliced
75 g crumbled feta
3 bacon rashers, cooked and diced
50 g pine nuts, roasted
100 g roasted red capsicum (pepper), sliced into strips
Barbecue rub (see page 164)
50 ml olive oil
salt and pepper, to taste
honey lemon mustard dressing (see page 160)
spiced avocado yogurt dressing (see page 160)

Rub the lamb back straps with oil and Barbecue rub let marinate for 30 minutes then on a hot grill cook for 3–4 minutes each side then rest for 10 minutes.

Prepare both the dressings and put them in the fridge until required.

Peel and cube the sweet potato place in a large bowl then microwave for 4–5 minutes until tender, dress with an enough oil to coat the potato and season with salt and pepper. Then place in a shallow oven tray on a medium hot Barbecue with the hood down for 10–15 minutes or until browned once done set aside.

On a medium hot barbecue cook off the bacon to your liking and set aside to dress the salad later.

Slice the lamb back strap into thin slices then on serving platter add the leaves, onion and toss, then top with the lamb slices, sweet potato cubes, beetroot, feta, capsicum and bacon.

When ready to serve top with both the honey lemon mustard and spiced avocado yogurt dressing and pine nuts.

LAMB RISSOLES

Serves 6

---

500 g lamb mince
1 small onion finely diced
½ cup breadcrumbs
¼ cup diced sweet chargrilled capsicum
1 egg
1 clove garlic finely chopped
1 teaspoon ground cumin
¼ bunch fresh mint, finely chopped (keep some for garnish)
spray oil for cooking

Place the mince, onion, breadcrumbs, mint, garlic and cumin in the bowl and combine.

Season with salt and pepper.

Divide mince mixture into 6 portions the shape each portion into a patty.

Heat barbecue plate or chargrill over medium-low heat. Spray both sides of rissoles with oil. Cook, turning occasionally, for 12 to 15 minutes or until cooked through.

Serve on platter or make a burger.

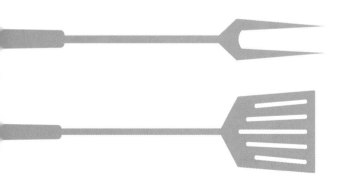

GREEK LAMB SLIDERS

Makes 12

---

500 g ground/minced lamb
1 small onion, finely diced
1 clove garlic, minced
1 teaspoon ground cumin
1 teaspoon ground coriander
1 egg
1 teaspoon chilli flakes
(optional)
salt and pepper, to taste
1 tablespoon olive oil
1 Lebanese cucumber, finely
sliced with vegetable peeler
Garlic mayonnaise
2 Turkish pide loaves,
cut into 12 rings

Using a cookie cutter, cut out rounds from the bread to create your slider buns.

Place mince in a large bowl and mix together with the onion, garlic, cumin, coriander, egg, chilli flakes, if using, and season with salt and pepper. Roll into small balls and flatten the patties to fit your buns.

Prepare barbeque for direct-heat cooking. Heat until hot. Oil the grill bars, cook the lamb for 3–4 minutes each side or to your liking.

To assemble your sliders, add some lettuce to the bun, a cooked patty then a slice or two of tomato and cucumber.

Finally, add a dollop of Garlic Mayonnaise. Place the bun on top and hold everything together with a cocktail stick.

Serve them while hot.

LAMB DONER KEBABS

Makes 18-20

1½–2 kg boneless lamb, forequarter or leg rolled roast
¼ cup fresh lemon juice
¼ cup olive oil
2 teaspoons freshly crushed garlic
1 teaspoon oregano leaves
1 tablespoon finely chopped fresh mint
½ teaspoon ground black pepper
1 teaspoon salt or to taste
soaked cotton kitchen string for tying

FILLING

2 tubs prepared hummus dip
1 head lettuce, finely shredded
4 large tomatoes, thinly sliced
2 large onions, thinly sliced
1 tablespoon chilli sauce
3 packets large Lebanese flatbread

Untie the joint and open it out. Place the skin side down in a flat, non-metallic dish. Mix the remaining lamb ingredients together, spoon over the surface of lamb to cover and allow to marinate for several hours in the refrigerator. When ready to use, reroll and tie with the soaked kitchen string.

While lamb is marinating, prepare all the filling ingredients and when required transfer to the barbecue area.

Prepare a covered barbecue for indirect-heat cooking over medium-high coals, reducing to medium during cooking. Preheat gas barbecues to high and turn to medium when the meat is placed on. Insert a drip tray.

Place the lamb roast on greased grill bars over the drip tray. Close the lid or hood. Cook for 1¾–2¼ hours, turning the roast after 40 minutes. The roast will be ready when the juices run clear when pierced with a skewer or when an inserted meat thermometer reads about 70°C for medium-well done. Remove the roast, cover with foil and rest 15 minutes before carving.

Carve into thin slices, keep warm. Place the flat breads over the grill bars to heat. Spread the flatbread with hummus, top with lamb slices and salad ingredients and drizzle with chilli sauce. Roll up and wrap a paper napkin around the end.

AT THE **BBQ** WITH

MERV HUGHES

It's all about good beer, good food and great mates.

Timing

Timing can be crucial. So the routine is, you get the sausages on for the kids and the guys that want an entrée. That gives a little bit of fatty cover over the barbecue. A lot of people don't like doing that because they reckon the sausage taste goes into the steak. But if you give it a bit of a scrape down, and there's a little bit of oil left on plate, it's perfect.

Pop your prawns on because they're an entrée dish too.

Put your steak or lamb on and slow, slow cook your meat. Turn the burners down low and slow cook it. Only turn your steak once.

Then get your chicken or fish on.

When you're doing a sit-down barbecue lunch or dinner you don't want people staggered when they're eating. You want everyone sitting down together so basically the steaks go down first and then the chops, if you've got any chicken or seafood, put them on last because they obviously cook quicker.

Dream Barbecue Guests

If I'm hosting a barbecue and I'm inviting people around, I'd be lying if I didn't say I'd love to invite Leroy Jethro Gibbs (Mark Harmon) from NCIS. I don't want Mark Harmon there, I want *Jethro Gibbs*. Then I'd have to have Aaron 'Hotch' Hotchner (Thomas Gibson) from Criminal Minds. Those blokes are fantastic police. I watch them Tuesdays and Thursday nights and they always solve the crime in an hour. They clean it up, how good are they? So if anything goes wrong at the barbecue I know they can sort it out within an hour, so they're good people to have on board.

I'm an Aussie rules tragic so I'd have to invite Doug Hawkins, Scotty Wynd and Chris Grant from the old Footscray Bulldog days. If you invite those three you can't go without Brad Johnson and Rohan Smith. They've just gotta be there. Then there's cricket. I don't know where to pull up on the cricket so I better invite every player I've played with. I just really enjoy their company but I'd definitely have Swampy (Geoff Marsh), Tubby (Mark Tayler), Heals (Michael Healey) and AB (Alan Border).

And that's the thing about good mates. You might not see them for four or five or six years but then you sit down, you have a beer and a steak and it's just like yesterday. There's no pressure, there's no dramas. That's what good friends are.

KRANKSY HOTDOG

Serves 6

---

6 Kranksy sausages
6 hot dogs rolls of your choice
cheddar, Swiss or
provolone cheese, grated
caramelised onion relish
(see page 178)

Slice the Kranksy sausages in half lengthways but not all the way through. Place on the barbecue grill for 3–4 minutes on each side until heated through.

Place the Kranksy on the bread roll and top with the cheese and onion relish.

 MERV'S TIP

Add other toppings as you wish, such as sweet coleslaw or red cabbage and apple slaw.

BARBECUE ROASTED LOIN OF PORK

Serves 4

800 g boned loin of pork
¼ cup sun-dried tomato pesto

Honey and chilli marinade

¾ cup barbeque sauce
½ cup sweet chilli sauce
2 tablespoons honey
1 tablespoon peanut oil
salt and pepper

Tie the pork loin with kitchen string at 25 mm intervals to keep it's shape when cooking.

Rub the sun-dried tomato pesto over the surface of the roast. Prepare the barbeque for indirect heat, medium hot.

Place the loin over the drip pan, cover with the lid or hood and cook for 50 minutes.

Mix the marinade ingredients together and glaze the pork every 10 minutes for a further 45–55 minutes – total cooking timeis approximately 1¼–1¾ hours. If you are using a meat thermometer, the inside temperature should reach 75–77°C.

When cooked, wrap the pork in foil and stand for 15 minutes before carving. Slice the roast and serve with vegetables of your choice.

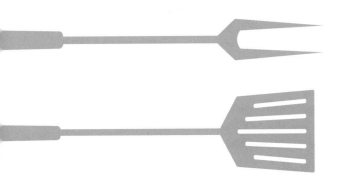

SPICY PORK SLIDER

Makes 12

2 tablespoons hoisin sauce
(Chinese barbeque sauce)
3 tablespoons dark soy sauce
2 tablespoons shaoxing wine or
dry cooking sherry
salt, to taste
¼ teaspoon Chinese five spice
1 teaspoon chilli flakes
(optional)
¼ cup brown sugar
1 teaspoon red food colouring
(optional)
2–3 pork (tenderloins) fillets
12 slider buns of your choice
1 cos lettuce (or any lettuce
you prefer), torn
2–3 tomatoes, thinly sliced
char siu sauce, to serve
plum sauce, to serve

Mix the Hoisen, soy, wine, salt, five spice, chilli flakes, sugar and red food dye in a shallow dish big enough to lay your fillets in.

Place the fillets in the dish and turn the fillets to coat. Cover with cling wrap and refrigerate overnight if possible or at least two hours.

Place the fillets on rack into a prepared barbeque for indirect cooking at 180°C, cooking for 40 minutes, turning after 20 minutes. Brush the fillets occasionally while cooking with the leftover marinade. Remove and rest, before slicing thinly.

Slice the burger buns in half lengthwise. Add lettuce to the bottom half of the buns, add a piece of pork or two to each bun. Top the pork with either mustard, char siu or plum sauce and add a slice of tomato. Hold the sliders together with cocktail sticks and serve hot or cold.

GRILLED BEER DOUGH PIZZA WITH SPICY ITALIAN SAUSAGE AND SWEET PEPPERS

Makes 4 pizzas

1 tablespoon olive oil
4 spicy Italian sausages
2 large red onions, sliced
2 large red capsicums
(peppers), halved and cut into
1 cm slices
125 g grated gouda cheese

Heat the oil on a medium—hot barbecue flatplate. Squeeze out the sausage meat from their skins into roughly 2 cm chunks. Cook until charred and cooked through.

Meanwhile, add the onion and capsicum to the barbecue and cook until soft.

To prepare the pizza dough (see page 150).

 MERV'S TIP *The less toppings, the better.*

MARINATED BARBECUE PORK CHOPS

Serves 4

4 pork chops

Marinade

3 tablespoons soy sauce
3 tablespoons worcestershire sauce
3 tablespoons hoisin barbecue sauce
1 tablespoon balsamic vinegar
1 teaspoon garlic powder
1 teaspoon onion powder
salt and pepper, to taste

Trim the pork chops of rind and excess fat.

Place all the marinade ingredients into a large zip-lock bag. Add the pork chops and marinade for 1–2 hours or longer if possible.

Heat the barbecue grill, then cook the chops for 5–6 minutes on each side. For crosshatch grill marks, turn 45 degrees after 3 minutes.

Turn down the grill and baste with the leftover marinade until the chops are cooked through. When done, cover with foil and rest for 5 minutes before serving.

Serve with a red cabbage and apple slaw (see page 129).

TERIYAKI PORK SKEWERS

Serves 6—8

1½ kg boneless shoulder of pork
1 cup Teriyaki sauce
350 g potatoes, peeled and cut
350 g sweet potatoes, peeled and cut
1 teaspoon freshly chopped chilli
1 tablespoon butter
1½ cups Greek-style yoghurt
8—10 bamboo skewers, soaked in water for 30 minutes

Cut the pork into 25 mm cubes. Place the cubes in a bowl and pour over the sauce to coat well, but keep a little to brush with while cooking. Cover and marinate in refrigerator for 1—2 hours or overnight to tenderise.

Cook the potatoes in boiling salted water. Drain well and mash. Add the chilli and butter and mix. Add extra butter if needed to make a fluffy mash.

Prepare the barbecue for direct-heat cooking and heat to hot. Turn a gas barbecue down to medium-hot when food is placed on. Set the pot of mash at the cooler side to reheat.

Place the pork skewers on the grill. Cook, turning and brushing with extra sauce for 12—15 minutes or until cooked to your liking.

To serve, pile mash in the centre of individual plates and top with the skewers. Drizzle yoghurt over the pork and season liberally with cracked pepper. Serve with a salad.

SPICED PORK KEBABS

Serves 4

---

500 g lean pork
1 tablespoon ground cummin
¼ teaspoon cayenne pepper
1 teaspoon dried parsley
1 teaspoon dried oregano
2 tablespoons olive oil
couscous, to serve

Soak 8 skewers in water for 1–2 hours. Cut the pork into 2cm cubes. Combine the cummin, cayenne, parsley and oregano. Rub the spices evenly into the pork and thread onto the skewers.

Lightly brush the skewers with oil before and during cooking. Cook on a lightly oiled barbecue on medium- high for 5–6 minutes (turning 2–3 times) or until the juices run clear when pierced with a skewer.

Allow the pork to rest for a few minutes before serving.

Serve on a bed of couscous.

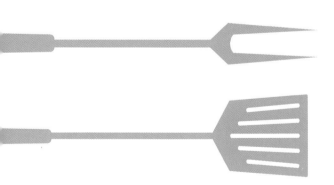

CURRY YOGHURT CUTLETS

Makes 12

½ cup natural yoghurt
1 cm piece ginger, grated
1 tablespoon lemon juice
2 cloves garlic, crushed
2 teaspoons curry powder salt
and pepper to taste
12 lean lamb cutlets
natural yoghurt, to serve

Preheat a barbecue to high.

Combine the yoghurt, ginger, lemon juice, garlic, curry powder and salt and pepper to taste. Marinate the lamb cutlets in the mixture for 10 minutes.

Barbecue cutlets for 3–4 minutes each side, depending on their thickness. Serve with natural yoghurt.

Chicken tenderloins can also be used in this recipe.

MERV'S TIP

To make a yoghurt dipping sauce, combine freshly chopped mint and a little chutney with natural yoghurt.

CRUMBED PORK FILLETS

Serves 6-8

---

2 pork fillets, about 450 g each

Crust Topping

2 cups fresh white breadcrumbs

60 g butter, melted

1 teaspoon freshly crushed garlic

½ tablespoon fresh oregano

1 tablespoon fresh basil, finely chopped

1 tablespoon fresh parsley, finely chopped

salt and pepper, to taste

1½ tablespoons pine nuts, toasted (optional)

1 egg

Remove any silverskin from the fillets, easing it off with a small sharp knife. Trim off the tapering ends from the fillets. Cut each piece across into 3 even pieces about 7 cm, depending on length of fillet. Place the fillet pieces in a well-greased shallow baking tray.

Combine all the crust topping ingredients except the egg. Beat the egg well and add just enough to moisten the crumbs. Divide the mixture and press a portion evenly onto the surface of each fillet portion.

Prepare the barbecue for indirect-heat cooking. For charcoal heat to medium high; for gas heat to high and turn to medium when food goes on.

Place the tray with the fillets in over indirect heat and cook with lid or hood down for 25–30 minutes or until done to your liking.

Remove the tray, cover and rest the meat for 5 minutes.

CHAPTER FIVE

SALADS & SIDES

CAESAR SALAD

Serves 4

2 baby cos lettuce, broken
30 g croutons
4 bacon rashers, diced
100 g shaved parmesan
4 boiled eggs

Dressing

2 tablespoons mayonnaise
1 garlic clove, crushed
1 teaspoon worcestershire sauce
1 teaspoon Dijon mustard
3 tablespoons lemon juice
salt and pepper, to taste
125 ml light olive oil
25 g finely grated parmesan cheese

To make the dressing, add all of the ingredients except the oil and cheese to a food processor. Blend, adding the oil in a slow stream. Continue until the dressing thickens, then stop and add the cheese and pulse until combined.

Break up the lettuce into small pieces and place into a serving bowl. Add the croutons, bacon, Parmesan cheese and boiled eggs.

Top with the dressing just before serving.

 MERV'S TIP *Keep the dressing for up to 1 week in an airtight container in the fridge.*

PEARL COUSCOUS SALAD

Serves 4–6

---

170 g pearl couscous
400 g tinned four-bean mix
2 large tomatoes, deseeded and diced
1 cucumber, peeled, deseeded and diced
1 small red onion, diced
¼ teaspoon salt
½ teaspoon cracked black pepper
2 tablespoons olive oil
3 tablespoons balsamic vinegar

Heat 250 ml of water in a saucepan over high heat until just at a high simmer. Add the pearl couscous and cover, simmering, for about 10 minutes. Stir every couple of minutes. The grains will fluff up just slightly and should be *al dente* when cooked. Splash with some of the olive oil and stir to coat the couscous so it does not stick together.

Drain and rinse the four-bean mix. Place the bean mix in a large bowl along with the pearl couscous, tomato, cucumber and red onion. Season with salt and the cracked black pepper.

Add the olive oil and balsamic vinegar and mix until all of the ingredients are combined. Place in the fridge until ready to serve.

RED CABBAGE AND APPLE SLAW

Serves 4–6

---

1 small red cabbage, shredded
2 granny smith apples,
julienned
½ small red onion, finely sliced
1 small bunch flat-leaf parsley

Dressing
3 tablespoons whole-egg
mayonnaise
3 tablespoons sour cream
3 tablespoons cider vinegar
1 teaspoon Dijon mustard
1 tablespoon honey
salt and pepper, to taste

Combine the cabbage, apple and onion in a large bowl.

In a separate bowl, mix together the mayonnaise, sour cream, vinegar, Dijon and honey and season to taste.

Add the dressing to the slaw and toss well. Garnish with parsley. Refrigerate until needed.

 *Make up the day before for better taste and texture.*

SWEET COLESLAW

Serves 4—6

1 small head cabbage, shredded
2 carrots, peeled and grated
1 red onion, finely sliced

Dressing

250 g whole-egg mayonnaise
3 tablespoons apple cider
3 tablespoons sugar
salt and pepper, to taste

Combine the cabbage, apple and onion in a large bowl.

In a separate bowl, mix together the mayonnaise, cider and sugar and season to taste.

Add the dressing to the slaw and toss well. Refrigerate until needed.

 MERV'S TIP *Make up the day before for better taste and texture.*

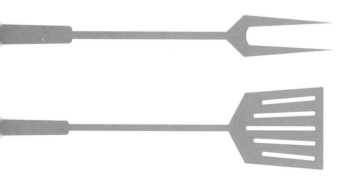

CAJUN CHAT POTATOES

Serves 4

500 g chat potatoes
4 tablespoons olive oil
2 tablespoons Cajun seasoning
(see page 163)
2 teaspoons salt

Wash the potatoes well and cut them in half. In a large bowl place the potatoes, olive oil, Cajun seasoning mix and salt. Toss to coat thoroughly. Place the potatoes into a baking dish and cover with foil.

Place the dish onto the barbecue grill plate and cover or pull down the barbecue lid. Check the potatoes to make sure they don't stick to the bottom of the dish. The potatoes will take 20–25 minutes to cook. Test with a skewer.

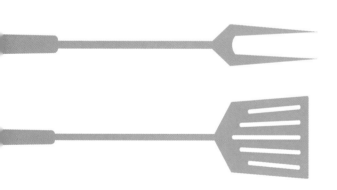

PLUM-GLAZED CHIPOLATAS IN A BASKET

Serves 4

1 kg chipolata sausages
½ cup sweet plum marinade
(see page 170)
1 bread basket made from a
cobb loaf

Leave the sausages in links, place in a skillet with water to just cover. Bring the water slowly to a simmer then remove from the heat, cover and stand until the sausages are cool. Drain well, separate the sausages and refrigerate in a sealed container until needed.

Heat the grill bars or grill plate on a barbecue using direct heat to medium-high. Pour the marinade into a small skillet and place on the grill to heat. Remove to the side when heated.

Place a sheet of baking paper over the grill bars or plate and the arrange sausages in rows. Working left to right, cook the sausages, brushing with the plum marinade and turning frequently until cooked and well glazed.

Create the bread basket by cutting the top off of a heated cob loaf and hollow it out to create a bowl. Transfer the sausages to the bread basket. Place on a platter with extra marinade served separately. Provide cocktail picks for serving. Invite guests to tear bits off bits of the bread basket as it empties.

SWEET POTATO WEDGES

Serves 4—6

2 large sweet potatoes,
scrubbed and cut into wedges
3 tablespoons olive oil

Seasoning mix

1 tablespoon coarse salt
1 tablespoon paprika
1 tablespoon chilli powder
1 tablespoon cracked black
pepper

Make the seasoning mix by combining the salt, paprika, chilli powder and cracked black pepper.

Placed the potato wedges in a large bowl, add the olive oil and toss until all of the wedges are coated in oil.

Sprinkle with the seasoning mix (reserve some of the seasoning to garnish at the end) and toss again until the wedges are well coated with seasoning.

Place the wedges on the barbecue grill on a medium heat for 30 minutes, turning every 5 minutes. When cooked a knife, will pass through the wedge easily.

Place the wedges on a serving platter and garnish with the remaining seasoning mix to serve.

GREEK SALAD

Serves 4

---

2 English cucumbers, sliced
4 Roma tomatoes, quartered
2 red onions, quartered
85 g feta, crumbled
½ cup Kalamata olives,
left whole
3 tablespoons extra-virgin
olive oil
2 tablespoons red wine vinegar
pinch of sea salt
freshly ground black pepper,
to taste
2 tablespoons oregano leaves

Place the cucumber, tomatoes, onion, feta, and olives in a bowl.

Whisk together the olive oil and vinegar in a separate bowl. Pour the dressing over the salad, then season with salt and pepper.

Garnish with oregano leaves. Serve the salad on its own or with fresh bread.

BALSAMIC VEGETABLES

Serves 6

2 large zucchini (courgette)
1 red capsicum (pepper)
1 yellow capsicum (pepper)
1 green capsicum (pepper)
3 beetroot
1 large eggplant (aubergine)
2 red onions
2 tablespoons balsamic vinegar
2 garlic cloves, crushed
2 tablespoons thyme
2 tablespoons basil
3 tablespoons olive oil
balsamic glaze (see page 164)

Cut all of the vegetables to equal size. Place on a lightly oiled, medium high grill until lightly browned and have a grill marked appearance. Place in a foil BBQ roasting tray lined with baking paper.

Combine the balsamic vinegar, garlic, thyme, basil and oil in a bowl and whisk.

Add the dressing to the vegetables and toss to coat.

Place the tray on a medium-high barbecue grill and close the lid. Roast, tossing every 5–10 minutes, until golden and tender.

Dress with the balsamic glaze and serve.

GRILLED ASPARAGUS

Serves 4

2 bunches asparagus
3 tablespoons olive oil
salt and pepper, to season
balsamic glaze (see page 164)

Snap off the woody part of the asparagus, then toss in the olive oil.

Cook the asparagus on a medium-hot barbecue grill for 2–3 minutes, then turn over and cook for a further 2–3 minutes or until charred and tender.

Serve on a platter and drizzle with balsamic glaze just before serving.

MERV'S TIP *You can also use store-bought balsamic glaze.*

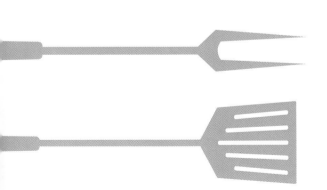

CUCUMBER SALAD

Serves 6-8

---

3 cucumbers, washed, dried and thinly sliced
1 tablespoon salt
2 garlic cloves, cut into slivers
175 ml balsamic vinegar
2 tablespoons sugar
freshly ground white pepper, to taste
1 tablespoon parsley or fresh dill, chopped, to garnish

Arrange the cucumber slices in a deep bowl and sprinkle with salt. Cover with a small plate that fits inside the bowl and place a heavy weight on top. Set aside at room temperature for 2 hours.

Place the garlic slivers in the vinegar and set aside for at least 30 minutes.

Drain the juice from the cucumber; squeeze the cucumber as dry as possible. Add sugar and pepper to the garlic-flavoured vinegar and pour over the cucumber. Taste and adjust the seasoning, if necessary. Cover tightly and chill thoroughly.

Before serving, drain the vinegar from the cucumber and sprinkle the dish with chopped parsley or dill.

AT THE
BBQ
WITH
MERV HUGHES

**A beer & the barbecue
go hand in hand.**

Essentials for a Ripper Barbecue

It goes without saying you need good sausages and steak, a good set of tongs, a spatula and beer. Of course, you also need a barbecue.

I think about who is coming, what I am going to cook and how many I need to plan for. Then about an hour before people start showing up I'll do the shopping.

I'm a bloke. You don't want to be too organised. As long as you've got an idea of numbers and how many kids are coming, you're sorted.

Kids love sausages, rissoles and chicken skewers. The big kids love prawns. I like to do an array of meat too. Lamb chops are always good. I love lamb chops, especially the big fatty tail but it's not good for my heart!

Beer

When you go to the butcher to get your meat, make sure you drop in and get a box of beer. I like to work to the ratio of a box of beer to every steak.

A barbecue is a great reason to drink beer. Most people barbecue in the summer and in the summer most people like to have a cold ale on the go.

I'm not one for really sticking with one brew. I chop and change but I am really into my craft beer. There is one I am particularly fond of which is 7.5 per cent alcohol. That one sorted me out up in Darwin last year. I thought I could handle it but my behaviour proved otherwise.

I always encourage people to have a cold beer while they're cooking a steak and when they're enjoying the barbecue meat with a salad. A glass of wine doesn't go astray either.

Moustache Etiquette

The one dish I normally steer clear of – for obvious reasons – is soup.

You can't cook soup on a barbecue so I'm pretty safe however sauces and marinades are probably my biggest enemy when it comes to the moustache.

I tend to reach for the barbecue sauce and I've got to be careful with that. Tomato sauce, for some reason, blends in better. And white sauce is a no go.

I must admit I do chilli prawns on the barbie and they're really spicy. I really love them so I have to wrestle with the chilli sauce at times, it really gets caught in the moustache.

BARBECUED SMASHED BABY POTATOES

Serves 4–6

1 kg new baby potatoes
2 tablespoons olive oil
salt, to season
2 tablespoons rosemary and garlic seasoning (halved to use before and after cooking)

Add the whole baby potatoes to a large saucepan of salted water over medium heat. Bring to the boil, then reduce to a simmer. Cook for about 20 minutes, or until a fork can be pushed through with no resistance.

Drain the potatoes. Once they are cool enough to handle, place on a chopping board and smash each potato being careful to keep them from breaking apart to much.

Place in a large bowl, and dress with the olive oil, salt and seasoning.

Place the potatoes on a hot barbecue grill and cook for about 5 minutes on each side, or until lightly browned and crisp.

Remove the potatoes to a platter, sprinkle with the remaining rosemary and garlic seasoning and serve immediately.

CHILLI BUTTER CORN COBS

Serves 6

---

6 sweet corn cobs, in their husk
250 g butter, softened
2–3 jalapeños, finely diced
1 red onion, finely diced
½ bunch coriander, finely chopped
½ teaspoon pepper

To prepare the corn, pull the silk off but leave the husk on (don't break off). Carefully rewrap the husks arranging it around the cob, then tie the ends with cotton kitchen string.

Soak the corn in a bowl of water for 30 minutes.

Preheat the grill to medium–high heat and grill the ears for 10-15 minutes. Pull the husk back and continue to grill on a lightly oil brushed grill, turning occasionally, until the kernels are tender and charred in spots (about 10 minutes).

Combine the butter, jalapeños, red onion, coriander and pepper. Place the butter in fridge if required.

Once cooked, lather the corn with the chilli butter and serve.

GRILLED BEER DOUGH GARLIC CHEESE PIZZA

Makes 4 pizzas

355 ml can beer (whatever you are drinking will be fine)

2 teaspoons dry yeast

315 g bread flour, plus 3 tablespoons extra, for rolling

1 teaspoon sugar

1 teaspoon salt

2 tablespoons olive oil

parmesan, garlic and parsley butter (see page 175)

3 tablespoons grated cheese

MERV'S TIP *You can prepare a few pizza bases in advance, just put baking paper between them and store in a cool place to stop them from rising again.*

In a bowl, pour in the warm beer and add the yeast. Let it stand for about 10 minutes to activate the yeast.

In another bowl, add the flour, sugar and salt. Slowly add the beer mixture to form a dry dough. Add a little more flour or beer if needed. Knead to form a nice elastic dough ball.

Place the ball into a large bowl that has been coated in the oil and rub some over the ball as well. Cover with a tea towel and then let the dough rise for about 1 hour, or until roughly double its original size. Knock down the dough and divide into 4 pieces depending on how big you want your pizzas. Roll into balls and cover with a tea towel and rest for a further 10–15 minutes.

Take a ball and roll out. The shape doesn't matter as it doesn't need to be round. Brush a thin coat of olive oil on one side. Place the dough on a hot barbecue grill, oiled side down, and leave for about 3 minutes. Using tongs, lift the edge to see if it has nice grill marks. Then flip it over to grill the other side.

Brush with melted parmesan, garlic and parsley butter and extra cheese. Close the lid on the barbecue (or take inside and put in a hot oven if you don't have a lid). When the cheese is melted to your liking, it's done.

Cut into slices and serve while warm.

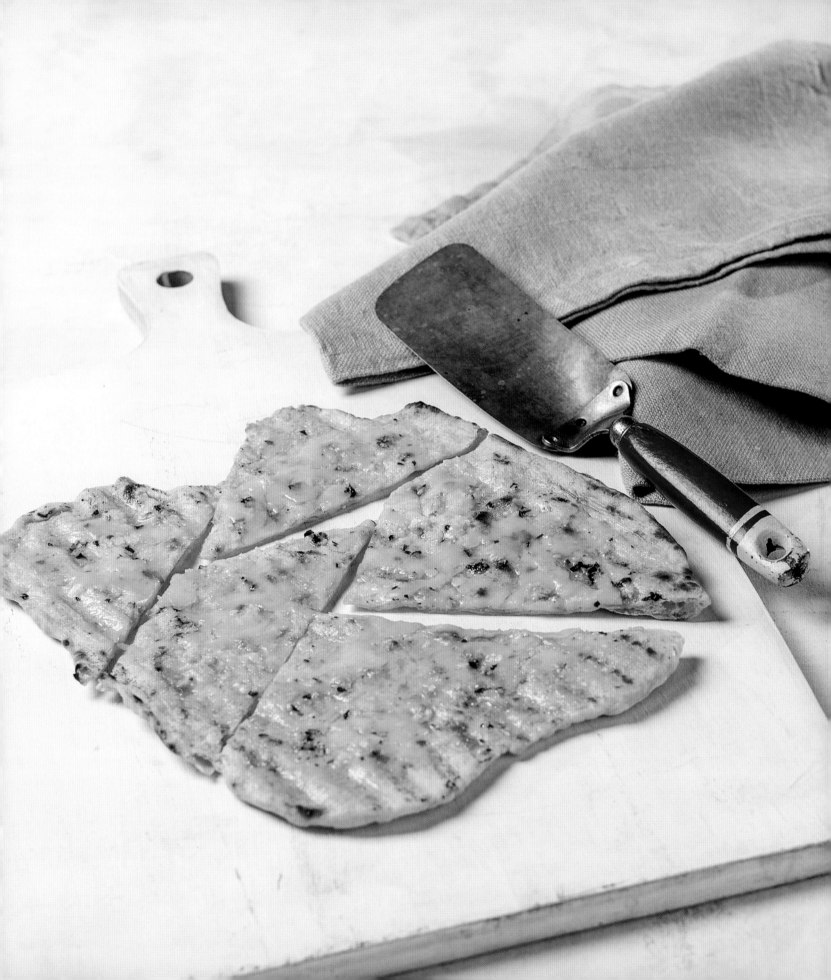

STUFFED JALAPEÑO CHILLIES

Serves 3—4

12 jalapeño chillies
100 g grated
cheddar cheese
250 g cream cheese
50 g bacon, finely diced
12 small bacon strips, to wrap
over the top of the chillies

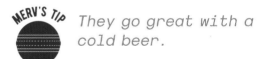

MERV'S TIP *They go great with a cold beer.*

Cut the tops off the chillies and de-seed (a apple corer works quite well, gloves are a good idea also).

Lightly brown the diced bacon on a medium high hot plate. Allow the bacon to cool. Combine the cheese and diced bacon.

Put the cheese mixture in a plastic bag and cut the corner off. Fill each jalapeño with the mixture and place a strip of bacon over the top to seal using a toothpick.

Place upright on a chilli board and place over medium—high barbecue grill for 10—15 minutes, or cooked to your liking.

POTATO SALAD WITH BACON AND BOILED EGGS

Serves 6

1.5 kg chat potatoes, whole and unpeeled
3 bacon rashers, rind and excess fat removed and diced
185 g sour cream
125 g whole-egg mayonnaise
1 tablespoon wholegrain mustard
1 small red onion, finely diced
1 bunch chives, finely chopped
salt and pepper, to season
4 hard-boiled eggs

MERV'S TIP *Use cooking scissors to chop the chives.*

Put the potatoes in a large saucepan, cover with water and pinch of salt. Place the saucepan over medium heat and bring to the boil. Reduce the heat and cook the potatoes until tender. Once the potatoes are cooked, drain and let them steam dry. Once cool to the touch, quarter.

Meanwhile, cook the bacon in a frying pan over medium heat until crispy. Remove the bacon from the pan and drain on paper towel.

In a small bowl, mix together the sour cream, mayonnaise, wholegrain mustard and onion.

In a serving bowl, add the potato and combine with the sour cream and mayo mixture. Sprinkle with the bacon and chives. Top with the boiled eggs.

HOT POTATO CAKES

Serves 4–5

---

800 g potatoes, peeled
1 tablespoon butter
¾ cup sour cream
1 teaspoon chopped chives
¼ cup plain flour
¾ teaspoon baking powder
dill, finely chopped, to serve
sour cream, to serve

Boil the potatoes until tender, drain and mash. Stir in the butter, sour cream, chives, our and baking powder. Form into patties using about ¼ cup of mash for each. Place onto a tray, refrigerate until ready to cook.

Prepare barbecue for direct-heat cooking. Heat the grill plate to hot and oil well. Place the potato cakes on the grill, cook until brown on both sides. Keep warm.

Serve with a dipping bowel of sour cream and garnish with dill.

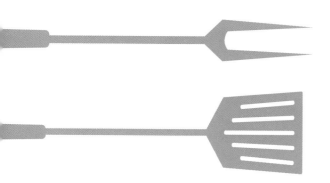

CHAPTER SIX

DRESSINGS, RUBS & MARINADES

HONEY LEMON MUSTARD DRESSING

juice of ½ a lemon
2 tablespoons honey
3 tablespoons olive oil
2 tablespoons Dijon mustard
salt and pepper, to taste

Add all of the ingredients to a small jar and shake to combine.

Note: Store for up to 7 days in an airtight container in the fridge.

SPICED AVOCADO YOGURT DRESSING

juice of ½ a lemon
½ avocado
2 tablespoons chopped flat-leaf parsley
½ teaspoon coriander powder
salt and pepper, to taste
125 g Greek-style yoghurt

In a blender, add all ingredients except for the yoghurt. Blend until smooth, then add the yoghurt. Stir to combine. Refrigerate until needed.

ROSEMARY AND GARLIC SEASONING

5 g dried rosemary
2 teaspoons garlic powder
2 teaspoons onion powder
1 teaspoon black peppercorns
1 teaspoon salt
Using a spice or coffee
grinder, grind the rosemary and
peppercorn into a powder.

In a small bowl, combine all of the ingredients.

Note: Store in an airtight container for up to 6 months.

CAJUN SEASONING

2 teaspoons paprika
1 teaspoon salt
1 teaspoon black pepper 2
teaspoons garlic powder
2 teaspoons onion powder
1½ teaspoons dried thyme
1½ teaspoons dried basil
1 teaspoon cayenne pepper
1 teaspoon chilli flakes
(optional)

Combine all of the ingredients. Add the chilli flakes if you like.

Note: Store in an airtight container for up to 6 months.

BARBECUE RUB

¼ cup brown sugar

2 teaspoons paprika

1 teaspoon salt

1 teaspoon mustard powder

1 teaspoon black pepper

1 teaspoon chilli flakes

1 teaspoon onion powder

1 teaspoon garlic powder

Combine all of the ingredients.

Notes: Store in an airtight container for up to 6 months.

Increase the pepper and the mustard to make it hot and spicy by adding a few more teaspoons.

BALSAMIC GLAZE

---

125 ml balsamic vinegar

50 ml tomato sauce

4 tablespoons barbecue sauce

½ cup brown sugar

1 garlic clove, crushed

1 tablespoon mustard

½ tablespoon cracked black pepper

Combine the ingredients in a saucepan and bring to boil then reduce to a low heat until it has reduced by half and is a thick consistency.

Note: Store in an airtight container in the fridge. Use as a glaze for asparagus, chicken or salmon when grilling.

Team Bonding

If someone on the team put a barbecue on, I was always keen to get over and join in. We never really used barbecues as an opportunity to get any issues with teammates out in the open. If you had any issues with anyone, they wouldn't be there!

There are not many opportunities for a barbecue when you're on tour. But we always knew where to hunt down a good steak.

It was easier to organise barbecues when we played in Australia. There was, I guess a bit of a routine as to where we were playing and what we'd get up to.

Swampy (Geoff Marsh), used to have a barbecue at his place on the Saturday night of the Perth test match. Tubby (Mark Taylor) and Tugga (Steve Waugh) hosted barbecues during the Sydney test match or after a One Day International.

Sydney was normally at the back end of the tour so the barbecue arrangements would be in place early. If you were in the side you knew the Saturday night was going to be barbie night. You locked it in.

If someone goes to the effort to put a barbecue on, you turn up. And you certainly go and take full toll. You take full advantage of it. Barbecues are a lot of fun.

Out of Swampy, Tubby and Tugga, it'd be a dead heat for Gold medal. All three put on a good spread and there's always a good time to be had. You're with the rest of the team and if the players had their wives or family in town, they're always included.

If someone had a barbecue on anywhere there wouldn't be too many players in the side who would miss it.

AT THE
BBQ
WITH

MERV HUGHES

Nothing says bonding like a barbecue.

SATAY MARINADE

½ teaspoon ground ginger

½ teaspoon ground coriander

¼ teaspoon ground cumin

½ onion, grated

2 tablespoons peanut oil

1 teaspoon freshly crushed garlic

¾ cup roasted peanuts, puréed into a paste

2 teaspoons tomato paste

¾ cup creamed coconut

3 tablespoons honey

¼ teaspoon salt

Tip all the spices into a dry skillet and fry gently, stirring constantly until they begin to be aromatic. Remove from the heat and continue to stir for another minute. Add the grated onion and quickly combine.

Return to the heat and add the peanut oil. Gently fry the spices and onion for 3–4 minutes, then add the garlic. Fry for 1 minute, then add all other ingredients. Simmer for 10 minutes.

Allow to cool, then transfer to an airtight container. Makes approximately 2 cups in finished volume. Can be stored in the refrigerator for approximately 1 week.

SWEET PLUM MARINADE

1¼ cups plum conserve

¼ cup sugar

1 small red chilli, finely chopped

2 whole star anise

1 tablespoon Worcestershire sauce

1 teaspoon salt

juice of 1 medium lemon

¾ cup water

2 teaspoons corn flour

Put the plum conserve into a skillet. Add all other ingredients except ¼ cup of water and the corn flour. Stir to combine and simmer for 5 minutes.

Add a little of the water to the corn flour and work to a paste. Add the rest of the water to the corn flour and then add to the plum marinade. Stir to combine and simmer for another 5 minutes.

Allow to cool. Remove the star anise and transfer the marinade to an airtight container. Can be stored in the refrigerator for approximately 6 weeks.

SMOKY BARBECUE MARINADE

1 tablespoon smoked paprika

2 tablespoons brown sugar

2 garlic cloves, finely chopped

¼ cup golden syrup

1 tablespoon white wine vinegar

1 tablespoon olive oil

2 tablespoon barbecue sauce

In a mixing bowl, combine paprika, brown sugar, garlic, golden syrup, white wine vinegar, olive oil and barbecue sauce and mix well.

MERV'S TIP

This one's great to go on just about anything when you want an extra hit of flavour!

RUM AND BARBECUE SAUCE

---

1 teaspoon olive oil
1 small onion, finely grated
2 garlic cloves, crushed
250 ml tomato sauce
1 tablespoon soy sauce
1 teaspoon mustard powder
55 g brown sugar
125 ml spiced rum

Add the oil, onion and garlic to a small saucepan over medium heat and cook until the onion is transparent.

Add all the remaining ingredients, except the rum, and bring to the boil. Simmer for 20 minutes. Remove from the heat, then add the rum and stir. Allow to cool.

Note: Store in an airtight container in the fridge for 1–2 weeks.

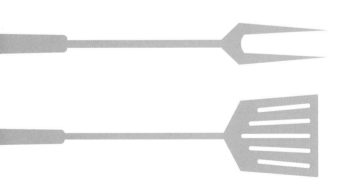

PARMESAN, GARLIC AND PARSLEY BUTTER

100 g softened butter
3 tablespoons finely grated
parmesan cheese
1 garlic clove, crushed
2 tablespoons chopped
flat-leaf parsley
salt and pepper, to taste

Mix the ingredients in a bowl until smooth. Place the mixture onto a piece of plastic wrap and roll into a tube shape, twisting the ends and tie.

Place in the freezer until firm, then cut into slices just before use.

LEMON GARLIC HERB BUTTER

100 g softened butter
finely grated zest of 1 lemon,
plus 1 teaspoon of juice
1 tablespoon finely chopped
shallot
1 tablespoon finely chopped
flat-leaf parsley
1 garlic clove, crushed
salt and pepper, to taste

Mix the ingredients in a bowl until smooth. Place the mixture onto a piece of plastic wrap and roll into a tube shape, twisting the ends and tie.

Place in the freezer until firm, then cut into slices just before use.

Great spread over a fresh baguette and heated under the grill for easy garlic bread.

CHILLI BUTTER

100 g softened butter
½ long red chilli, deseeded and
finely diced
1 garlic clove, crushed
1 tablespoon finely chopped
coriander
zest of 1 lime, plus 1 teaspoon
juice
salt and pepper, to taste
1 tablespoon sriracha sauce
(optional)

Mix the ingredients in a bowl until smooth. Add the sriracha sauce, if using, for colour and an extra kick.

Place the mixture onto a piece of plastic wrap and roll into a tube shape, twisting the ends and tie.

Place in the freezer until firm, then cut into slices just before use.

Note: Keep in the freezer for up to 1 month.

CARAMELISED ONION RELISH

1 tablespoon olive oil
2 red onions, sliced (not too thin, as they will burn)
3 tablespoons balsamic vinegar
½ cup brown sugar
1 teaspoon chilli flakes
1 teaspoon chives

Heat the oil in a large frying pan over medium heat. Add the onions, then reduce the heat to low–medium. Cook for 10–15 minutes, or until tender.

Add the balsamic vinegar, sugar and chilli flakes. Cook for further 15–20 minutes, or until the onions are a rich brown colour. Remove from the heat and cool.

Serve in a bowl garnished with chives.

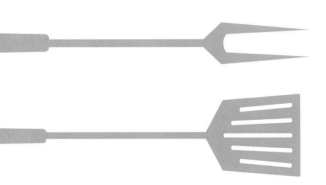

About the Author

Mervyn Gregory 'Merv' Hughes, the maverick former Australian cricketer, was born in Euroa, Victoria on November 23, 1961.

The right-arm fast bowler synonymous with his big moustache, represented Australia between 1985 and 1994 in 53 Test matches, taking 212 wickets. He played in 33 One Day International matches, taking 38 wickets.

An Australian sporting legend, loved by cricket fans around the world, Merv made his debut for Australia against India in 1985–1986. He took a hat trick in a Test against the West Indies at the WACA in 1988–89, and went on to take 8-87.

Over six tests in the 1993 Ashes tour, Merv took 31 wickets from almost 300 overs, helping Australia to a 4-1 victory over England. He was a talented lower-order batsman, scoring two half-centuries in tests, and over 1000 runs in all.

A serious knee injury sustained during the 1993 Ashes tour saw Merv make a fleeting Test comeback the following summer, before finishing with his 212 career wickets.

Hughes replaced former Australian cricket captain Allan Border as an Australian selector from 2005-2010 and continues today to be involved in cricket at both an elite and junior level.

Aside from cricket and AFL, Merv's other passion is fishing.

INDEX

Thank you to Brooke & Justin Taylor for allowing Merv to be photographed in their beautiful Sydney home and to Trenton International Hotel & Restaurant Supplies for helping to make Merv's food look delicious.

First published in 2017 by New Holland Publishers

London • Sydney • Auckland

The Chandlery, 50 Westminster Bridge Road, London SE1 7QY, United Kingdom
1/66 Gibbes Street, Chatswood, NSW, 2067, Australia
5/39 Woodside Ave, Northcote, Auckland, 0627, New Zealand

newhollandpublishers.com

A record of this book is held at the British Library and the National Library of Australia.

ISBN 9781742576121

Group Managing Director: Fiona Schultz
Publisher: Monique Butterworth
Project Editor: Gordana Trifunovic
Proofreader: Kaitlyn Smith
Merv Hughes Photographer: Sue Stubbs
Food Photographer: Rebecca Elliott
Stylist: Gabrielle Wheatley
Food Consultant: John Cowie
Designer: Catherine Meachen
Production Director: James Mills-Hicks
Printer: Hang Tai Printing Company Limited

10 9 8 7 6 5 4 3 2 1

Keep up with New Holland Publishers on Facebook
facebook.com/NewHollandPublishers